The Art of Walking

The Art
of Walking

Sonia Overall

Shearsman Books

First published in the United Kingdom in 2015 by
Shearsman Books
50 Westons Hill Drive
Emersons Green
BRISTOL
BS16 7DF

Shearsman Books Ltd Registered Office
30–31 St. James Place, Mangotsfield, Bristol BS16 9JB
(this address not for correspondence)

www.shearsman.com

ISBN 978-1-84861-448-2

ACKNOWLEDGEMENTS

blacked-out reveries
from a page of Rousseau, 'The Confessions of J.J. Rousseau',
trans. 1783.

labyrinths
discovered text from Borges, 'The Garden of Forking Paths',
trans. D. A. Yates.

I
method

précis

It is simple and soon you will be running. But now
you must make those tentative trails, the one   two   o n e
and expect to trip.
This is just a beginning. First you must fall.

Once you have balance you may begin again. You are coltish, a
stripling. You are a swaying sapling feeling to the tips of fine-
fibred roots and pulling them free. The ground is uneven. The
plane is littered with obstacles. You will learn to negotiate these.

Left. Right.

Left. Right. Find the rhythm. Grow taller. Take on speed.

Walk. Do this without thought, without effort. Walk as if your
feet were lungs serving their unconscious purpose.

Walk holding hands. Walk on low brick walls and high grassy
banks. Walk along the wet perilous perimeters of swimming
pools. Walk on the gnarled foundations of Roman villas. Stub
your toes on ancient hooks of flint.

Walk carrying lunchboxes in the shapes of animals. Walk carrying
satchels containing Latin text books, plimsolls and unfinished
homework in exercise books ruled with faint blue ink.

Walk carrying all of your worldly possessions in a bundle on a
stick, a dog nipping at your heels, your clothes in rags, laughing.

Walk in parks. Walk on beaches. Walk beside busy roads and attempt to negotiate traffic. Walk in supermarket aisles steering trolleys, avoiding contact.

Walk for pleasure, slowly. Walk to clear your head. Walk to fill it.

Walk in sunshine with head high, seeking birdsong in trees, blinking in the light. Walk in rain under percussive umbrellas. Walk into high winds, gasping, shedding garments. Walk in sackcloth under raining blows, head bared, guilt-ridden.

Your soles thicken. Your legs fold like poorly-hinged gates. Your ankles soften with fluid. Your knees buckle. Take a seat. Allow your feet to rest on cushioned stools. Attach wheels to furniture, to stationary objects, to high-sided chairs. This is an ending: allow others to walk. Just watch.

contained, linear

Measure your right foot. Use a ruler, a wooden one, preferably yellow. (Your old school ruler is best.)

Work in inches. The body does not conform to metrics.

Place your left foot at the starting point. Imagine a chalked line on the floorboards. Step forward onto your right, heel to toe.

Waver: balance. Repeat.

Remember: you are not measuring distances. You are taking in perimeters.

Keep going, heel to toe to heel to toe and do not be tempted to pick up speed or fidget or fudge at corners for precision is vital and this is not about velocity or momentum so do not give in to the distraction of speed but stop

stop

and wait for the balance again. Now proceed, methodical.

Tortoise-like, you begin to understand vastness, the space of the shell and the space beyond the shell.

Do not stumble into meditation – that is for later. Remember that this is an experiment and should be conducted with absolute focus and rigour.

Consider the ditches around your paddock. Consider the walls of wire mesh around your pen. Consider the volume they encompass.

Complete the circuit and come to rest at the starting point, one foot hovering in accordance with perpetual motion.

Now complete the equation to determine the contained area in square feet.

To achieve the cubic volume, walk up the walls.

(If you forgot to count, return to step one.)

inverted

There are stars in the grass. You feel these with outstretched fingers. Your nails root in the soil, tickling the soft bodies of seeking worms. Your palms flatten. Your toes spring skywards. Your wrists beat with pressure, your knuckles rise and fall like viaducts.

Your fused calves are an arching whip above your torso. Your pointed feet are a hovering scorpion sting.

You look the laced boots of your companions humbly in the eye as you recede, a scraping suitor, from their presence.

You are a diver. The horizon swallows you.

subliminal

Do not look down. You have no need of maps. The path is sinking sand beneath shallow waves. You keep the world on your left, the sea on your right.

This is the street. You simply feel it. At the corner is the abandoned grocers, shutters down. The sign is illegible; you do not need the sign.

You need no compasses. Your feet swim below you. You sense the quiet ticking metal of parked cars, the distant reversing of vehicles, the whirr of passing bicycle wheels.

You cross the street. Your ankles describe the inclines of curbs, the distinctness of grass and gravel. The house peers above a bib of white-pebbled driveway, fat-cheeked, pink, stippled.

You no longer notice how ugly it is. You no longer notice the yellowed newspaper against the porch glass, the abandoned milk bottles, the layers of weather.

You open the door, remove your skin, hang it on the coat hook.

retreat

Go. Do it swiftly, hand at mouth, marvelling. Do not look back.

Paper darts will rain at you, each point perfectly folded, the creases sharp, the words within sweetly plosive, seeking. Do not commit the shapes to memory, repeating them silently in the night, testing them on your tongue.

Go. Go before the fragile shoes shatter beneath your feet. Hesitate, and grind glass fragments with your heels, waltzing the crazed pieces into pebbles.

Stop, and you will find yourself kneeling at a grate picking peas and lentils from ashes, said from unsaid, truth from text. Unhook those tugging barbs, the tender tendrils reaching for your ankles, the slow ambush.

Go. Believe in the midnight carriage, the wheels carrying you to an absolute ending.

promenade

You expected to be part of it: a human tide swarming the shoreline. Instead you stand apart to watch the slow progress, the select following a slivered beacon.

The electric spoke is precisely a mitre's length. More or less.

The sky roses. The sea is a patch of poorly printed crosshatch.

You would walk out, salted soles skating glassy waves. But the pier is shorter than you thought, its distant bulbous dome the disconnected dot of an i. An island.

You wait, faithful. The lights flash. You might have joined them, might have been a torchbearer. But there is no signal.

The air is chill and heavy. Your toes numb.

They do not call out for you.

You make your own promenade, humming home, a rattling goods van on the rails, *a thumb of rum and a warm bed. A thumb of rum and a warm bed.*

(a)symmetrical

The path narrows
forcing you into separateness.
You would reach for a steadying
elbow but
there is no room here for touch,
the blank windows of the
terraces
too close.

This is stolen time,
adrenaline thumping weight
into your hinges.
The tarmac crackles with it.

You sink into chairs
flanking the hard pool of
tabletop
the shape of a warning sign.
Grateful,
you wear your weariness
like an old blanket.
It settles into your folds.

It settles into your folds
like an old blanket.
You wear your weariness,
grateful,
the shape of a warning sign
flanking the hard pool of
tabletop.
You sink into chairs. The tarmac
crackles with it,
adrenaline thumping weight
into your hinges.
This is stolen time.
Too close,
the blank windows of the
terraces:
there is no room here for touch.
You would reach for a steadying
elbow, but,
forcing you into separateness,
the path narrows.

intervention

It is March, or April, a Sunday.   Wet.   Bottled.   All of
summer to come.

You twitch around the house until the sky lifts.

Onto the lawn then, six o'clock sounding from the
steeples as you   kick off boots peel away socks
spread thirsty toes into damp blades of green.   Worm
casts ooze.

By the bottom gate behind twisted cox and chicken
coop you run   run in circles   faster and faster
grass tangling clinging –

in the morning, fleshy parasols of a fairy ring spread and
shiver there. From the window you follow that track,
one fingertip dipped in condensation, living out loops of
unformed leaf and letter.

non-corporeal

a blackbird cuts across the grid of window and
                              within the room
you continue the call and response
following the apertures of small interests
        the opening and closing remarks
        the chases and cul-de-sacs of conversation
waiting for the black dart of wing to reprise

already your thoughts have stretched their arms   risen
                              sought coats and boots
leaving you for the broad avenue smelling of rain and
                              impending night
the stark trees stencilled against pasteboard sky
where day fades faster than they can walk
        (thedyingbatteryofanoldtorch light)

leaving your body in the muffled room
                to fend for itself

in the rain / departure

leaving, door wedged open

water pooling, you step into the rain

filaments of longing curling

like burnt hairs

you turn up your collar

late train / arrival

Moist-mouthed o of moon bright as a streetlight. Frost
sequins concrete.

Leaf shadows on the path a willow-pattern. You are the
figure on the bridge, stooped as hope, low satchel
bruising right thigh.

Behind you the train-gates raise, release.

Not a soul on the street. Fox scent planted in crevices
like white-man's-foot. Jack-by-the-hedge early to
flower, bolting.

These late nights home. Every mile a long-drawn
breath. You taste the salt of it, pull out your key and
falter: foolish legs folding beneath you, iron girdles
crashing into the sea.

II
psychogeography

lost: Placa de la villa Gracia

You are waiting it out in the only cafe in the Gracia that
doesn't serve cerveca.

You were looking for a September Revolution but ended
up with pigeons, Catalan voices and a zodiac clock
tower.

There are too many kissing couples.

Not a word of English – thank god – but across the
square is the *Romeo & Juliet* and the mopeds race like
any small-town Friday.

When the sax player sputters into *My Way* you call for
la cuenta and keep on searching, fold away map and
guidebook, a Lucy without her Baedeker.

Pézenas

six o'clock in the labyrinth of Pézenas

and you can buy a glace or a souvenir plate

but the cafés are closed

up the steep lanes and through

the mouse hole arch

of seven centuries

from behind the silent shutters of the old ghetto

the smell of something roasting:

this is what it means to be elsewhere

Good Friday in Perpignan

les veilles réligieuses
veiled, shouldering mysteries
and bobbing peaks of penitents

footsore, you peel away from the procession's tail
to snake through the back streets
slithers of houses, four storeys
of balconies swagged with washing

a cock crows from a darkened stairwell

you sit at a canopied café in
the Place de la Révolution
where the gecko fountain spits
and the boys line up the pressions

a bent woman, black burkha and begging bowl
corners the square
you finger the clasp of your purse
pas ici! calls madame

she shuffles on, smiling

relief swells
you sip your coffee and finally notice
that the piped hymns from the loudspeakers
have cycled around

the boys call for another round of beers
c'est belle says the man
at the next table
to nobody in particular

skating to Dover

the next station is
                Shepherdswell –

if you dared you could get out now
watch the taillights judder to dim distance
let your eyes feed the grey April ten o'clock   bruised
                                    purples navy olive
your heel crunching platform

crouch down
inch yourself to the edge and
lower in:

shallow end
rails steely slick
snaking parallels
chin level   bags shouldered
slow-footing into giant skis
until you feel the tick and rhythm
and you skate   grace   speed

railings strobing
tremulous flick of lighted islands
ditches sidings hamlets outhouses
open-sided barns

              Kearsney –

skirting tributaries and buried springs
lakes where lovers' names are whispered to bulrushes
discarded glass shards   fish scales   salt eddies
shelled oaths   fox barks   nettle patches
piled timber of storm-felled trees
empty fields bearing dips and scars
mansioned titles   razed monasteries and courtyards
                                        forgotten shames and battlefields
blinking into the tunnelled glare of

              Dover –
end of the line
edge of the world

Margate, 5th May

You make a pilgrimage to Hamish Fulton's milestones and full-moon walks. Old straight tracks and forced courses. In the cube of the gallery you shuffle at the perimeter, safety in short distances, your own termite walk. You feel as if you are participating.

An object cannot compete with an experience. Even so, you linger over the smuggled Tibetan flag, hungry for reliquary.

You are enamoured with text. There is a pleasurable hollowness in your belly, like the spaciousness after a fever. Then a toddler breaks in, squeals at the giant red SILENCE on the wall, gleefully stamps in orange boots. You realise that *she* is participating.

The tide is high, swollen by twelve days of rain. The harbour arm struggles to contain it.

Flitting between galleries, you think: there is as much in a straight-trodden line as in any Turner firebomb. Visitors cluster before a furnace. No matter how you resist you are drawn to the light, the slow goosestep of the figurative.

That night your dreams are of levitation, of a marching bass, of an endless single line of yellow road-paint cutting through the Downs.

if the ant insists

on marching   across my papers

I   will write   a   poem

around

it

blacked-out reveries

body and mind embellish nature

wandering lover

obliging little caresses, looks

apprehension walked on lightly

youthful desires filled the houses

wanton walks

voluptuous mountains

pleasure of going no where

labyrinths

in the middle of the fields
                take the road to the left
at every crossroads turn again
to the left
        steps slowly tangled

the usual procedure

the hand of a stranger
           the secret crest of a mountain
                      provinces and kingdoms
                  one sinuous spreading
          intimate   infinite

confused meadows
          syllabic music of the wind dimmed by distance
              fireflies
           streams of water
      a tall, rusty gate
the house within
      a lantern
      a face

blinded language

the garden of forking paths
      long   low   calculated

tireless interpretation
      chaotic manuscripts
           contradictory symbols

      barbarous   irretrievable
every one imagined

intricate territories

the confusion of the maze
the curious legend tenuous and cross-sectioned
a cyclic volume whose last page is at the middle
               word for word
                     on to infinity

confronted with several alternatives simultaneously
         diverse futures proliferate the point of
departure

resign yourself

within the vivid circle of the lamplight
                  a growing, dizzying net of
        divergence

innumerable futures
           secret, busy and multiform
      dissolved along the path

mappa mundi

Begin wherever the arrow falls

        you may need chalk to mark perimeters
           where land and sea meet

borders are not barriers to progress

        but stepping on cracks is as crossing continents
           (they do things differently there)

crossroads are perfect places to loiter
and bargain for wares, souls or melodies

        but beware deep woods, wolves, witches in trees
      ditches where bodies may roll, bandits, brothers who
                prove false,
       lovers likewise, and be sure never to take the

left hand fork

skirt about the hems of lakes
avoid dipping toes in rivers
never board a boat with blackened sails
block your ears when the singing begins

        but walk: walk until you meet a man
         who asks questions of your oars
              your eyes
          or your intentions

and stop there.